FAMILIES AROUND THE WORLD

A family from BOSNIA

Julia Waterlow

WAYLAND

FAMILIES AROUND THE WORLD

A family from **BOSNIA**

A family from **BRAZIL**

A family from **CHINA**

A family from **ETHIOPIA**

A family from **GERMANY**

A family from **GUATEMALA**

A family from **IRAQ**

A family from **JAPAN**

A family from **SOUTH AFRICA**

A family from **VIETNAM**

The family featured in this book is an average Bosnian family. The Bucalovics were chosen because they were typical of the majority of Bosnian families in terms of income, housing, number of children and lifestyle.

Series editor: Katie Orchard
Designer: Tim Mayer
Production controller: Carol Titchener

Cover: The Bucalovic family outside their apartment with all their possessions.
Title page: The Bucalovic family on their balcony.
Contents page: People waiting in line for water, in Sarajevo.

Picture Acknowledgements: All the photographs in this book were taken by Alexandra Boulat. The photographs were supplied by Material World/Impact Photos, and were first published by Sierra Club Books in 1994 © Copyright Alexandra Boulat/Material World. The map on page 4 is by Peter Bull.

First published in 1997 by Wayland Publishers Limited
61 Western Road, Hove
East Sussex, BN3 1JD, England

© Copyright 1997 Wayland Publishers Limited

Typset by Mayer Media

Printed and bound by Canale & C.S.p.A., Turin, Italy.

British Library Cataloguing in Publication Data
Waterlow, Julia
  A family from Bosnia. – (Families around the world)
  1. Family – Bosnia and Herzegovina – Juvenile literature
  2. Bosnia and Herzegovina – Social life and customs –
Juvenile literature
  I. Title
  306.8'5'094742
ISBN 0 7502 2024 4

Contents

Introduction

Former Yugoslavia

Bosnia was once part of a much bigger country called Yugoslavia.

REPUBLIC OF BOSNIA-HERZEGOVINA

Capital city:	Sarajevo
Size:	51,130 square kilometres
Number of people:	4,400,000
Main Language:	Serbo-Croat
People:	Bosnian Muslims 44%, Serbs 31%, Croats 17%
Religion:	Muslim, Christian (The Serbs belong to the Eastern Orthodox Church and the Croats are Catholic)
Currency:	Bosnian Dinar

THE BUCALOVIC FAMILY

Size of household:	5
Size of home:	60 square metres
Workweek:	0 hours (Adults are paid for civilian labour)
Most valued possessions:	Lokman: Medical book, radio; Nafja: Electric lamp
Family income:	About US$25 each month

The Bucalovic family is an average Bosnian family. The Bucalovics have put everything that they own outside their home so that this photograph could be taken.

Meet the family

1 Arina, mother, 26
2 Nedzad, father, 23
3 Nadja, daughter, 2
4 Lokman, grandfather, 67
5 Nafja, grandmother, 65

A COUNTRY OF CHANGE

Bosnia was once part of a country called Yugoslavia. Three main groups of people – Muslims, Croats and Serbs – lived there. When Bosnia became an independent country, these groups started fighting each other. The Serbs killed many Muslims or forced them to leave their homes.

On a dark night in November 1992, the Serb army attacked the Muslim town where the Bucalovic family lived. Nedzad, Arina and Nadja fled. After six hours walking they arrived at Arina's parents' home in the city of Sarajevo. All they had with them was the clothes they were wearing and Arina's handbag. They all went to live in Arina's parents' third-floor apartment.

'Life in Sarajevo is often very boring but then suddenly very scary.' *Arina.*

A home in Sarajevo

Arina's parents' apartment where the Bucalovic family lived. It has four small rooms and views of the hills around the city.

UNDER ATTACK!

In 1993, Sarajevo was surrounded and under attack from the Serbs. There was often bombing and shooting, and the buildings were hit by shells. The streets were not safe, so Bosnians used to spend a lot of time inside.

The Safest Room

The family's apartment had a living room that faced out on to the main street. The family didn't use the room much because it was on the side most likely to be hit by shells and bullets. Lokman built a barricade (made of shelves full of clothes, books and bricks) across the room so the bullets couldn't get through.

Most of the time the family stayed in the kitchen at the back of the apartment. Although it was rather dark, they felt safer here. Nafja and Nadja used to sleep in the kitchen. Lokman slept on the sofa in the living room, with Nedzad and Arina on a mattress on the floor beside him.

This room used to be Nafja and Lokman's bedroom. During the war it became a place where the family stored things.

Waiting for Light

After the war started, electricity and water only came on every now and then. So Nafja always kept her electric lamp switched on. The lamp was very important to her because when it came on, she knew the electricity was working. Then the family had light and could watch television.

Nadja sometimes helped her mother by filling the bath. This gave the family enough water for a few days.

'When the water was working, we had to fill the bath quickly. We never knew when it would stop working again.' *Arina.*

Nafja tried to keep warm and read although there was often no electricity.

Making Do

It can get very cold in winter in Sarajevo. After the gas was cut off, the Bucalovics' only heating came from a stove in the kitchen. They could not always get wood for the stove, so Lokman had an idea. He soaked paper and cardboard rubbish in water and squashed it to make hard balls. He left the paper balls to dry out on the balcony. He then burned these balls of paper in the stove.

Lokman used rubbish to make balls to burn on the stove.

▲ Nadja joins other people in the basement of the apartment block. This was the safest place to be when there was a lot of bombing.

When the bombing was bad, the Bucalovics and other families in the apartment block would shelter in a cellar under the building. Nadja's parents spent so much time in the cellar that they hated it. They stopped using the shelter altogether. Arina and Nedzad preferred to risk staying in the apartment. But they still sent Nadja down.

Food and cooking

HIGH PRICES

Because Sarajevo was under attack and surrounded by Serb forces, it was difficult for food to reach the city. Most shops were closed and there was not much food in the street markets. It was also very expensive – just one carrot cost US$3 and a kilo of meat US$32 – that's more than a month's income.

Instead of a gas cooker, the Bucalovics cooked on a wood-burning stove.

The family usually started the day with tea, cheese and bread. The baker's shop didn't always have bread, so often Arina or Nafja baked it at home. Nadja liked drinking milk but the Bucalovics couldn't buy fresh milk for over a year. Instead Nadja had dried milk, mixed with water.

An Evening Meal

Nedzad enjoys a good meal after coming home late.

One of the family's favourite dishes was tomato and onion salad. The Bucalovics had this with their main meal in the evening if they could find good food in the market. Arina or Nafja often used to cook the family a main dish made of rice, tinned meat and potatoes.

Fresh Food

With the war going on, any kind of fresh food, such as vegetables, fruit or meat was very difficult to find. The Bucalovics were given extra food by the United Nations every month. The United Nations gave them some oil, tins of meat and fish, flour, beans and sugar.

Arina walks round the market, looking for some fresh food.

Arina used to go to the market to look for potatoes and fruit. Sometimes she came home with nothing because food was too expensive or else not worth buying. Often the vegetables were too old and dried up to cook with.

'I used to grow roses on the balcony but you can't eat them. So I started growing tomatoes instead.' *Lokman.*

Working together

The family often had to collect water from a tap in the street. Arina used Nadja's baby carriage to carry plastic jugs to put the water in.

WARTIME JOBS

Everyone in Bosnia was caught up in the war and few people had normal jobs. Some were fighting and some were refugees. Others, such as doctors, helped in hospitals looking after the people who had been wounded.

Surviving

Lokman and Nafja helped around the house but they were too scared to go out. Lokman liked gardening on the balcony when it was quiet. This was risky because he could have been shot. Only Arina and Nedzad went out into the streets to get supplies.

Arina used to have her own shop before the war. But in Sarajevo she spent most of her time finding the basic things the family needed to survive. One of her jobs was to go and collect water when there was none in the apartment. She used to take lots of plastic jugs and load them into Nadja's baby carriage. She then walked two kilometres to a public tap to fill them. When she got home, Arina had to carry them all up to the apartment.

Arina queues at the tap in the street for water.

At War

For eight days at a time, Nedzad used to leave home to join the Bosnian army who were fighting the Serbs. He had to make a dangerous journey on foot into the mountains around Sarajevo.

Nedzad in his Bosnian army uniform.

Nedzad was a hairdresser before the war. During the war he liked to keep in practice by doing Nafja and Arina's hair. Both women liked to look as smart as possible even though they hardly ever went out. Nedzad did his best, even though there was no shampoo or hairdryer.

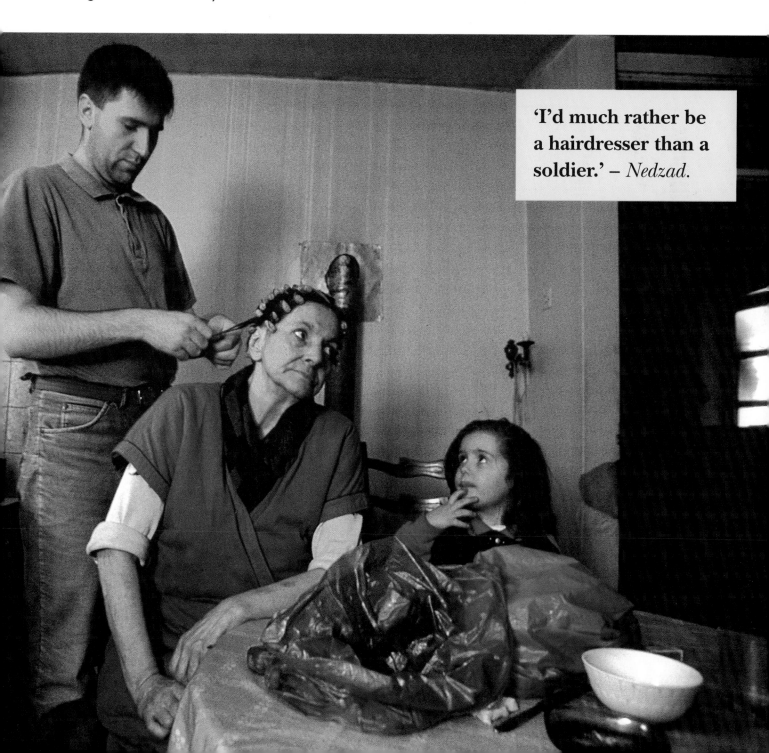

'I'd much rather be a hairdresser than a soldier.' – *Nedzad*.

Danger Outside

When Nedzad came back home from fighting, he used to help Arina to get food and wood. Often they couldn't go out because the city was being bombed by the Serbs. But when it was quiet, Nedjad and Arina set off to find supplies. Even then, shells or bullets suddenly hit buildings or people in the streets. They had to move very carefully, keeping behind buildings.

Nedzad fills his backpack with wood. He bought the wood from a friend.

Arina stored the wood that Nedzad bought on the balcony.

School and play

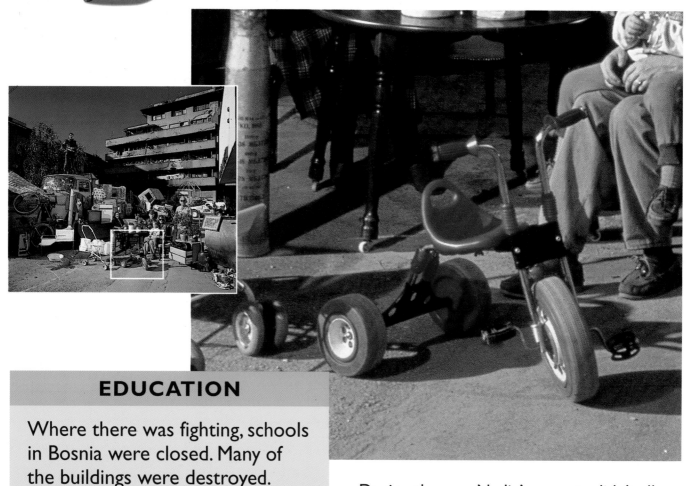

EDUCATION

Where there was fighting, schools in Bosnia were closed. Many of the buildings were destroyed. Before the war, Bosnians were well-educated – 88 per cent of women and 97 per cent of men could read and write.

During the war, Nadja's parents didn't allow her to ride her bike out on the streets.

Every morning during the war, Radio Sarajevo announced whether the schools would be open or not. Many had been bombed or else they were full of refugees. Sometimes it was too dangerous for the children to go to school. When a school was open, children of all ages often had to crowd into one room for their lessons.

> **'In this house there are two dangers: the war and little Nadja!'**
> *Lokman.*

Playing at Home

Nadja was too young to go to school during the war. Most of her time was spent in the apartment. Her parents did not dare let her go outside in case she got shot. Instead, Nadja played with other children inside the apartment block or sometimes out on the balcony.

Nadja used to play out on the balcony with the boy next door. They played soldiers with his plastic machine gun.

Time to relax

This radio was important to the Bucalovics. It helped to keep them in touch with the news.

DANGER

Before the war, many people in Bosnia used to have holidays at the seaside or travel to other countries nearby. During the war, most people couldn't even leave their towns or homes because of the dangers.

The Bucalovics had a car before fighting broke out and used to go on family outings and holidays. During the war all their spare time was spent around the apartment. Lokman liked to listen to the radio or read his favourite book.

Arina loved clothes and make-up. When she came to Sarajevo all she had was her handbag and what she was wearing – jeans, a pullover, a warm coat and a pair of shoes. A girlfriend gave her some other clothes to wear. But Arina missed being able to go shopping like she used to and buy new clothes.

When it was quiet in the evening, Lokman used to lie down and rest, or read by candle light.

Hope for peace

Life is getting better for the Bucalovic family. The shooting in Sarajevo has stopped and supplies of food are getting through. Arina and Nedzad want to leave Sarajevo as soon as they can. They want to start a new life, with a modern house and furniture. Most of all, they want Bosnia to stay peaceful.

Nedzad prays at the grave of a friend of his who died in the war.

'Sarajevo will never be the same.' *Nedzad.*

THE WAR IS OVER

A peace agreement has now been signed between the Muslims, Serbs and Croats, and Bosnia has held elections. Although the war has stopped, many Bosnians are sad and bitter because they have lost their families and homes.

Nedzad and Nadja are happy that the war seems to be over.

29

Timeline

1459	Bosnia becomes part of the Turkish Ottoman Empire. Many people become Muslims.
1877	Bosnia becomes part of the Austro-Hungarian Empire.
1914	Archduke Ferdinand is killed in Sarajevo. This leads to World War I.
1918–1929	Bosnia becomes part of the new Kingdom of Yugoslavia.
1945	Yugoslavia becomes a communist state. Muslims, Serbs and Croats in Bosnia live together quite peacefully.
1992	Bosnia becomes independent of Yugoslavia. Bosnian Serbs and Croats fight. Sarajevo is under siege.
1995	In December a peace agreement is signed.
1996	Elections take place.

Glossary

Barricade A barrier to stop harmful objects getting through.

Elections These are when people vote to choose their new leaders.

Grave A place where dead people are buried.

Independent country A country that rules itself and is not controlled by another.

Muslims People who follow the Islamic religion. Muslims in Bosnia are generally not as religious as they are elsewhere in the world.

Peace agreement This is an agreement made by different sides in a war to stop fighting.

Refugees People who have had to leave their homes because of war or other troubles and have nowhere to go.

Shells Exploding bombs that are fired from big guns.

United Nations An organization made up of countries around the world which works to bring peace and a better life for everyone.

Further information:

Books to read:

Don't Forget Us – I Come From Bosnia by Anita Ganeri (Watts, 1993)

Zlata's Diary by Zlata Filipovic (Viking, 1994). This is the diary of a 10-year-old girl living in Sarajevo during the war.

Organizations:

The following organizations have a selection of education packs, some of which include case studies of children around the world:

Action Aid, Chataway House, Chard, Somerset TA20 1FA Tel: 01460 62972

Oxfam, 274 Banbury Road, Oxford OX2 7DZ Tel: 01865 311 311

Save the Children, 17 Grove Lane, London SE5 8RD Tel: 0171 703 5400

Index